LIMINALITY

KANWARJOY SINGH

Made with ♥ on the Notion Press Platform
www.notionpress.com

Contents

Contents

Acknowledgements

.

In the pages of this book,
I honor the salient pillars of my life,
Mom and Dad....

Preface

I can't overlook this condition,
I'm tired of making this everyday decision
To be or not to be, liminality
this is a poet's condition...

1. One Last Cry

For my legs have now overgrown the bed,
Suddenly, the doorbell rang
but this time was nobody calling out for me
it was Osiris in reality, it came to set me free
to set me free from all those ties
from all my sins
all the beautiful lies
Take me to the promised land!
For I am destined to meet someone there
the mother of beauty or something named 'care'.

Well, this is me,
A man in life's tyranny
Perpetuity is what this pain seems to be
perhaps I guess it's time to go
perhaps this is me, I'll bid farewell to thou
what if I took the road not taken?
Will I find my sparkling beacon?
For I was born to serve all my life
enslaved to my obligations
trapped in these lies

However,
this darkness, the deepness
this makes me who I am
lurking deep inside me
is death's monstrosity
I'm vulnerable, I'm gullible
to life's atrocity
even in the dark, I feel myself light up again
even in the depths, I feel myself float in pain
but I wish to submit,
don't want to survive
For death
is what I'll relish
and the dark is where I'll thrive

I feel like the sea,
unfathomably lost
I feel like a tree,
infinitely paused
The air, the snow and perhaps the rain
floating, falling or flowing through this pain
there's more to life, they say
not in my way, dismay
I can't overlook my condition
I'm tired of making this everyday decision

To be or not to be,
this is a poet's condition

Unbeknownst to me,
why this soul of mine wants to die
These eyes of mine yearning to offer one last cry
One last cry,
A cry to die…

2. Seventh Life

The world is fair to those not born,
For they have yet to see what's out there in the dark
A cursed land,
on which the sun sets upon
With cluttered love and drained bodies
feelings of procrastination and delusional stories
Is this a life to live?
A life perhaps the seventh one
leaving you to wonder
what you could've, should've, would've done.

3. One art by Elizabeth Bishop (PARAPHRASED)

The art of losing isn't hard to master
It's somehow therapeutic,
Thou shall realise, thereafter
Mustn't give up
In a titbit loss or disaster
Thou started losing
the day he was christened,
by the deity master
Many losses shall come and go
Many of them shall steal your laughter
But in the end,
The art of losing isn't hard to master

An entitled, lovable human
Loses the child within his skin
Loses the young man, like it's a sin
Loses the gentleman, who again wishes
to begin
You've survived enough disasters

It's time to accept,

The art of losing isn't hard to master

4. Wintertime Woe-ness

Ooo!
the tickling feel silently stunned me
Too stumped to see, gloom struck upon me
What was it ? I pondered
I froze, Why?
I wondered

Soon,
The contentment I breathed
Gradually ebbed away
the hefty winter flow
enfeebled me, I dismayed away
An ominous atmosphere
I could sense it, 'twas coming
Came, the winter
It was anything but stunning

Perhaps, I do get it now
It's wintertime woeness
Beauty but dullness

It's wintertime woeness
So please be good,
sincerest November
Please be kind,
dearest December
Nocturnal and distress
It's wintertime woeness

5. Liminal Life

They say broken pieces,
create the most beautiful pieces of art
so here I am,
A shattered piece of this broken world
building up itself and
building poetry
in life's labyrinthine
in this strenuous tapestry
I try to make sense of life
rekindling its spark,
that I seem to have lost
in the nothingness of life
in it's liminality, in it's lies

I slightly blame Camus and Kafka
for awakening me,
to this absurdity
I thank both of them
for this invaluable courtesy
This paucity of calmness
soon turns into monotony
How long, how long

will I live through this quandary
to live or to die
Where is my serendipity?

6. I was doing fine , Then I met you

How can you say it's wine,
without even tasting chardonnay
How can you know I'll lose,
if you don't ever even want to play
How can you say I'll quickly go
Just because you don't want to stay
Just try me once,
I'm sure I can be the weekend
to your dull Monday

7. Tearing and Sleeping

You know what's best
It's when I silently cry
The river doesn't stop flowing
No matter how hard I try
if it doesn't pause, It's fine
Sometimes it hurts, I know
It doesn't matter anymore
The tears are old cold snow
But still,
sometimes I want it to stop, you know

From where the fires ignited
It pains rather much
I'll somehow endure it,
I have the tears gentle touch
But If there's a purpose
To my suffering,
To the silent pain
Just tell me, dear Algea
And I'll accept it
With pours of my rain

I'll still stick to crying,
Till I sleep dreamless
And meet the eternal oblivion,
Blissful but stygian
I'll just cry till I'm satisfied
And that is never
sleeping a sleep
Which is stygian forever

8. That Day

On that day,
the world felt very large
my body very empty
and the night very dark
On that day,
An emotions ocean
was lit on fire
with many words unspoken
On that day,
in the nonchalant world
I never felt stiller
many lessons learned
On that day,
with a silence so deafening
Could hear a heartbeat
wishing it to stop
more than anything
And on that day,
**I could feel each letter of the word
'HURT'**

9. Emerald's Betray

I liked her in green
for she was a beautiful emerald to me
precious and rare
in my heart, she'll always be
Only after seeing that gem
is when I can have a good night's sleep
we talked and talked for hours
apparently, the talks were deep
I promised I would keep
that emerald safe with me
Cherish her beauty,
handle it with care
but ours was a love that she didn't share

That night was crueler than life per se
that jeweller took my emerald
and ran away.
The clocks have turned,
many seasons passed
but still,
In a room full of gems, I'd stare at her

Till another jeweller came and took her away
and she became a character from a book
I'd read long ago,
A book with a cover, so grim and grey
with the beautiful title
'An emerald's betray' …

10. Sorry and Thank You

Yesternight,
I couldn't go off to the land of Nod
too occupied wondering
and contemplating amidst the chaos
I thought,
what those selected, chosen people did
in their cursed past lives
what and how many sins, did they participate in?
How many were they condoned for?
why do they suffer for something they did before?
For they had to live such a life
A life, one wouldn't call a life
A life, where one would prefer death
until their very last breath

I deeply, deeply wish
I lived in a world, lived in a place
where a thing like underprivileged, was unheard of
where everyone was free, light and gay
where to simply exist,
one didn't have to pay

where one shouldn't have to
sell their body, unwillingly
where one wasn't born to be speechless,
or with any other kind of disability

oh dear! , oh god!
why this torment?
why do I have to be the entitled one
and not them?
why not those who suffer indescribably,
utterly and painfully?
Only two things now, my blue heart can say
To you and to them, on this gloomy day
where 'you' is the almighty
and 'they' are the needy
***I'm sorry** -*
sorry to them and
I'm sorry but you failed
*and **thank you** -*
thank you for my life,
thank you, for they have paid

11. The Warmth of Winter but not Love

This winter

Many emotions, concealed

keep telling myself

I'll obliviously sleep

Whilst I found comfort through

Apricity

and a love that was deep

This winter,

I was tiresome and weak

With Christmas incoming

Several happy tears in my way

It's okay if we felt different

I'll just write my dismay

The mufflements and blankets

Will provide me

What you simply couldn't

It was the warmth of love

Understand ?, well you wouldn't

12. Why are your Poems so Dark? by Linda Pastan (PARAPHRASED)

Doesn't it feel empty with all this white?
Sometimes,
at the end of the tunnel
there isn't always light
Don't your eyes hurt,
in the bright absenteeism of the dark?
Mine frequently do
Black are the eyeballs too
but with only the white
you wouldn't wish to live through

Or did you mean to ask
"Why are you sad so often?"
Ask the moon,
Ask what it has witnessed
And then answer me too.

13. Insane For This Sane World

The yearning voice in me,

its despicable, ruthless

it does no good to me, yet still, I love it

if you ask me why, I tend to reply 'I am like this'

for I can't find another plausible reason

for my unwanted existence

It's ironic perhaps absurd that,

I adore digging my own grave

I feel like I'm drenched in opulence

the opulence of confidence

that's hazardous once in a while

and sometimes, as charming as it could be

It's not wrong,

if I find comfort in the deepest of depths

I mean no harm, but somehow it is what it is

My emotions though kept but unkempt

My love harsh but soft, My eyes sleepy yet awake

This is me, This is who I ought to be

Maybe in the next life,

I'll be happy with no mercuriality

Therefore, I wish my death to be the cause,
of the birth of a human
more responsible,
eloquent and content
than I ever was.

14. A Poet

Are you drunk?
They asked
I'm a poet, I replied
Why don't you sleep?
They asked
What is sleep, If it died
Often, I crave
for unique words, it seems
Pardon my insanity
I write everything I dream
Pardon my sanity
In this world insane
I'm a poet, for Christ's sake
Preferring red wine
Over champagne

15. Unfamiliarity -who is he?

I try not to,
upturn this smile
for what are my grievances
In front of theirs
but why is it my laughter
that temporarily impairs?

I look in the mirror,
I'm not myself
Unfamiliarity, I see
I'm not myself
It's hard to see the beauty
Incredibly deficit of it
Where did it vanish
In the depths of sorrow, didn't it?

There aren't rainbows that shine,
Or stars that align
Only plain humiliation
Death is my sign

Where is the old me?
Who is he?
He's not himself
I think he'll never be

16. Down In The Childhood Dumps

I Still remember, the 'cars honk' by heart
I had to,
that's what I've learned from the start
When we broke a glass
It made sure to break us
Thereafter, I lost interest
I lost interest in kissing in bliss,
'cause someone who loves you wouldn't do this

When we seemed to enter,
the house together
I made sure,
I'm the first one to enter
So I could hide my soul
behind the door
Or nervously cry
on the raggedy floor

Sitting in the park, on the moving swing
Watching parents with their happy children
Wondering what's it like
to have a real, real childhood
I often contemplate,
that I almost had the same
If it wasn't for the monster
that I couldn't tame
Last night too, I had a dream
Where you were the devil, I was the broken teen
Felt dejected, jilted and depressed
Nevertheless,
let the rest of it rest

17. These Will Be My Years

These will be my years
It's my time to shine again
Rejecting all the disparities
singing through the terrible pains
Washing away, all stale tears
Chanting the anthem,
the anthem of powerful prayers
I'll fasten my seatbelt,
for the ride of life ahead
But these will be my years
You'll wonder if you misread

Saying goodbye to many,
Pleasurably
Saying hey to some,
humbly
Beating,
the unbeatable emptiness
Bearing,
the unbearable sadness
carpe diem, every day

gathering my rosebuds while I may

The temptations I need to banish

Believing in my grit,

I will somehow manage

I'll be the anti-hero

I'll stop with all the pondering

It's my time to shimmer again

the goal is to leave them wondering

these will be my years ahead,

they'll wonder if they terribly misread

18. That Bird, My Solitaire

In the middle of the night,
walking by
I hear a muffled, little chirp
coming from towards the sky
The chirp,
It sounded familiar
I reckon I've heard it before
I turned back,
Couldn't let my patience
Win anymore

I looked behind and could see a light
A beauteous white creature
Alone in the middle of the night
It was a bird or something,
A solitaire,
it's exquisiteness
just drugged me over there

A delicate bright bird
Shining in the stygian sky
Gave me hope
Of something,
That's going to soon come by
In all of this obscureness
There was something there,
Something luminous
Incredibly glare

19. Overshared

It's funny how you think
This one thing defines me
I tend to overshare
Because my own shadows
confined me
I want to speak my heart out
Can't I?
Is that a crime?
It isn't my fault,
if I couldn't hear
a single text chime

20. Let It Go

What's left in enmity?
Sometimes, I whisper to my soul
I think I can carry on,
And overlook this little mole
Believing there's nothing left,
In desire
Nothing left,
In revenge
I shall not keep burning in flames,
That are already drenched

You're not my enemies,
just some old fraud friends
It's okay you never apologized,
But for what, it really depends
I'd rather forget you, than hate you
And confine myself
To places we haven't ever been to
It's okay,
After all, you were a human
I was just one of them,
Who simply couldn't understand you.

21. Old Nonchalant Days

Childhood,

'twas a beauty

'twas calm

'twas enchanting

One of a charm

Nonchalance flowed in the air

Illiterate, what was despair?

Life was oblivious,

Undoubtedly smooth

I long to be back there

my young, nonchalant youth

And by youth, I mean

Before I was ten

Unaware of, what, was, when?

22. My Salvatore

A flower that blossoms
In the dead bouquet
She's the mannequin
In my heart, I want to display
I'm enthralled,
by her exquisite beauty
Behind her enigmatic smile
are plenty of thoughts unheard
Rare a girl she is,
Her name's the most beautiful word

She's meant for me, I believe
I'll scream her name happily if I achieve
She's a feeling
that I particularly enjoy
I wish,
for her
I was the only source of inexpressible joy
The summers are hot,
but I've been cold without her
I shall never be found lacking
Lacking of love for her

She's the only reason I have some hope
Some hope left in my heart
I beg you to make haste, my dearest!
Or I would end up with
No hope anywhere, my sincerest!
My Salvatore
Bereft of your love
ciao amore!

Thank You

Dear Reader,

As you embark on the journey through the pages of my anthology, I extend my heartfelt gratitude for choosing to explore the depths of my poetic expression. Crafting each piece has been a labor of love, and your support to accompany me on this literary voyage fills me with gratitude and humility.

Thank you for allowing me to share my world with you.

With sincere appreciation,

Kanwarjoy Singh

"STRIVE, ENDURE AND LIVE THROUGH
LIFE THE POETIC WAY."

-Kanwarjoy Singh

COMPILED , EDITED AND WRITTEN
BY KANWARJOY SINGH